FRUIT & VEGETABLES

Colophon

www.rebo-publishers.com - info@rebo-publishers.com

Design, layout and typesetting: R&R Publishing Pty. Ltd., Victoria, Australia

Cover design: Minkowsky Graphics, Enkhuizen, The Netherlands

Proofreading: Jarmila Pešková Škraňáková, Joshua H. Joseph

ISBN 90 366 1608 5

FRUIT & VEGETABLES

fresh from the greengrocer into your kitchen for

creative cooking

Foreword

Through the ages, many people have been inspired to write poems and prose in praise of one of nature's greatest gifts to us. And who could blame them? Vegetables, more than any other food, provide virtually unlimited culinary inspiration and by far the most varied and abundant source of nourishment.

Today, in your favorite greengrocer, you will see before you the vast array of colors, shapes and vegetable varieties available, inhale the earthy aromas and perfumes, and immediately begin to conjure up a symphony of exciting dishes in your mind. Or you may discover a new vegetable and think to yourself, "What is this? What can I do with it? How do I cook it?" Happily, the answers that you seek are now at your fingertips. This book has been carefully designed to assist you in expanding your repertoire of fruit and vegetable cookery. The recipes are healthy and nutritious, easy to achieve, and delicious. You will find all of your requirements whilst you "one-stop vegetables" at your favorite greengrocer. Not all that long ago the choice of vegetables was quite limited. But today, all that has changed, mainly due to the influence of excitingly rich and varied cosmopolitan populations. For example, we can now choose from at least a dozen different types of lettuce. Twenty years ago there were only a few choices available.

And with more and more people travelling overseas and being introduced to new taste sensations, is it any wonder that when they return, they demand a greater variety and selection of fresh vegetables? So, the next time you are faced with a diversified display of tantalising possibilities, remember this book, and prepare to enter the gardens of Paradise.

Measurements

All measurements conform to European and American measurement systems. For easier cooking, the American cup measurement is used throughout the book.

tbsp = tablespoon
tsp = teaspoon
oz = ounce
lb = pound
°F = degrees Fahrenheit
°C = degrees Celsius
g = gram
kg = kilogram
cm = centimeter
ml = mililiter
l = liter

Serves **6 people**

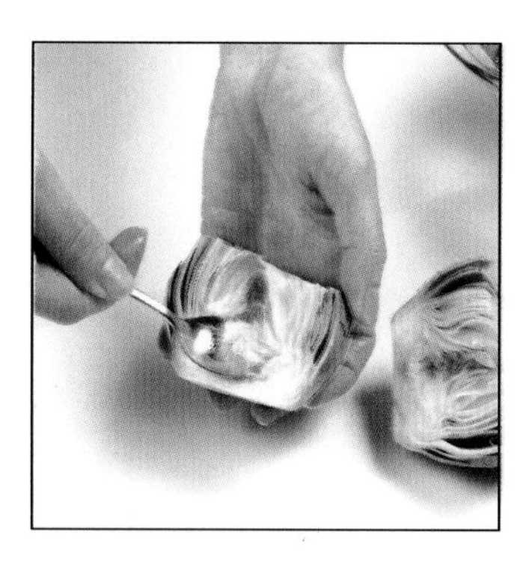

Prepare artichoke hearts. Strip away outer leaves, trim around base. Cut off top ⅓ of artichoke and cut in half. Scoop out furry center with tip of a teaspoon. Cut in half. Place in a bowl of cold water with a squeeze of lemon juice to prevent discoloring. Heat half oil in a large saucepan. Add green onions and saute until soft.

Crosscut root end of onions and place in saucepan. Add dill, carrots and potatoes, lemon juice, remaining oil, salt and pepper, and enough water to cover, then cook 15 minutes. Place artichoke halves over vegetables and cook 15 minutes more or until tender.

Remove vegetables to a heated platter with a slotted spoon, arranging attractively. Keep warm. Taste cooking liquid, add extra lemon juice and adjust seasoning if necessary. Stir in blended arrowroot and stir over heat to thicken sauce. Pour over vegetables. Serve hot with crusty bread as a main course.

Ingredients

6 globe artichoke hearts
½ cup olive oil
½ cup green onions, chopped
2 tbsp fresh chopped dill
1lb 2oz/500g baby carrots, scraped
12 pickling onions, peeled
12 small new potatoes
juice of 1 lemon
water
salt, pepper
2 tbsp arrowroot, blended
with a little water

Artichokes La Polita

Serves **2–4 people**

For the vinaigrette: measure mustard into bowl. Whisk in vinegar, sugar, salt, pepper, and herbs to taste. Continue whisking, slowly adding oil until mixture thickens. Set aside.

Remove the tough outer skin at the lower stem end with a vegetable peeler and trim the ends diagonally.

Steam asparagus by placing upright in a can half filled with boiling water. Stand in deep saucepan filled with boiling water halfway. Cover partly so some steam escapes, cook for 10-12 minutes or until tender, but crisp. Arrange on a plate and drizzle with vinaigrette. Serve warm or cold.

Ingredients

1 tbsp Dijon mustard

4 tbsp red wine vinegar

1 tsp sugar

½ tsp salt

½ tsp ground black pepper

finely chopped parsley and snipped fresh chives to taste

½ cup olive oil

1 bunch asparagus

Asparagus with Vinaigrette

Serves **6 people**

To make the sauce: whisk the egg yolks, mustard, and butter in a double boiler over simmering water, until mixture is frothy.

Add cream and mix for 3 minutes. Add vinegar. This can be set aside at this stage and reheated over simmering water when the beans are cooked.

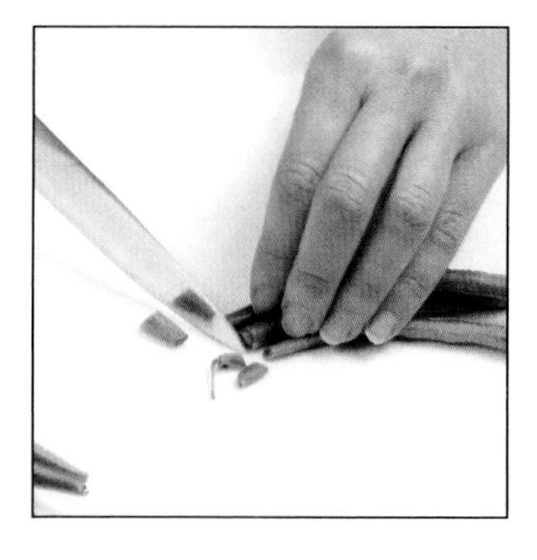

Wash and top and tail the beans. Steam until tender, but still crisp. Pour sauce over beans and serve.

Ingredients

1lb 2oz/500g green beans

3 egg yolks

1 tbsp French mustard

2 tsp butter

¼ cup cream

2 tsp vinegar

Green Beans with Mustard Sauce

Serves **4–6 people**

Wash bean sprouts. Top and tail beans and snow peas. Cut beans into 1¼in/3cm lengths and broccoli into small florets.

Heat oils in wok or frypan. Fry garlic for 2 minutes, then add beans and broccoli, stir-fry 3 minutes. Add baby corn and snow peas and stir-fry for a further 2 minutes.

Add bean sprouts, soy sauce, and chili sauce and toss until heated through. Stir in coriander and serve immediately.

Ingredients

9oz/250g bean sprouts

4oz/100g beans

4oz/100g snow peas

4oz/100g broccoli

½ can baby corn

1 tbsp vegetable oil

2 tsp sesame oil

1 tbsp soy sauce

2 tbsp chili sauce, or to taste

2 tbsp chopped fresh coriander

2 cloves garlic chopped

Stir-fried Bean Sprouts

Serves **6 people**

Cut off leaves and stalks ½in/1cm above the bulb. Wash the beets well. Place beets in a saucepan, cover with cold water and bring to a boil. Reduce heat to a simmer, cover and cook until tender, 40-50 minutes. Drain and rinse under cold water to cool.

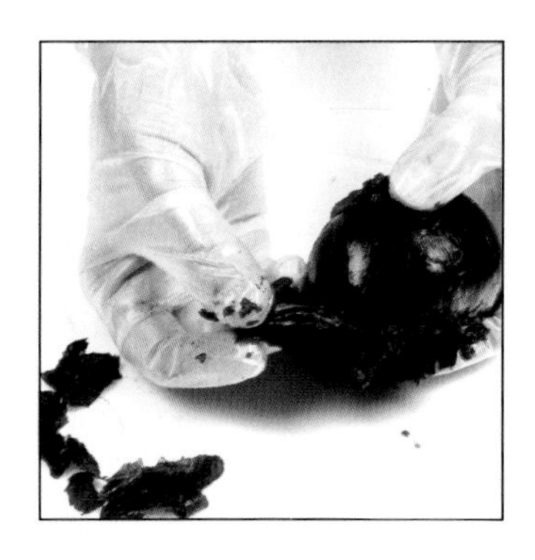

Remove the skin from the beets by pressing and sliding off with fingers. Wear gloves to prevent hands from staining. Cut into ¼in/½ cm pieces.

Combine sugar and cornflour in a small saucepan. Whisk in vinegar, orange juice, salt, and pepper. Whisk over medium heat until it boils and thickens, about 4 minutes. Whisk in the butter until melted. Remove from heat, pour over the beets and toss well. Serve hot or at room temperature.

Ingredients

2lb 4oz/1kg beets, well-rinsed

½ cup sugar

2 tsp cornflour

5 tbsp red wine vinegar

¼ cup fresh orange juice

salt to taste

freshly ground black pepper to taste

1 tbsp butter

grated zest of 2 oranges

Harvard Beets

Serves **4–6 people**

Cook broccoli florets in boiling water for 1-2 minutes, ensuring they are still crisp. Drain in a colander.

Heat the oil in a frypan. Cook anchovy fillets and garlic slivers, stirring until anchovies disintegrate. Add the chili and stir. Add cooked broccoli and pepper.

Meanwhile, cook the pasta in boiling, salted water until al dente. Drain the pasta and place in a large mixing bowl. Gently toss through the broccoli anchovy sauce.

Pasta with Broccoli and Anchovy Sauce

Ingredients

1lb 2oz/500g broccoli, cut into florets

4-6 anchovy fillets, drained

3 cloves garlic, peeled and thinly sliced

½ cup olive oil

½ tsp fresh chopped chili

ground black pepper to taste

14oz/400g pasta of choice

NICE
VERCHERIN & Cie

Serves **6–8 people**

Trim the base and remove any coarse outer leaves from brussels sprouts. Cut carrots into ½in/2 cm diagonal slices and leeks into ¼in/1cm pieces.

Place prepared vegetables into a saucepan of boiling salted water and cook until tender for 10 to 12 minutes. Drain well.

Meanwhile, melt butter in a small pan. Stir in the remaining ingredients. Toss well with hot vegetables and serve immediately.

Brussels Sprouts with Horseradish

Ingredients

1lb 11oz/750g brussels sprouts

3 large carrots, washed and peeled

3 leeks, washed and trimmed

2 tbsp butter

3 tsp horseradish cream

3 tbsp cider vinegar

1 tbsp finely chopped parsely

3 tsp fresh chopped dill

½ tsp salt

ground black pepper to taste

Serves **6 people**

Separate the cabbage leaves, wash and drain. Cut the thick rib from the leaves. Stock leaves and form into a roll then shred finely. Place the shredded cabbage, carrots, chives, pineapple, and pine nuts into a bowl.

Place the shredded cabbage in a large bowl and toss in the carrot, chives, pineapple, and pine nuts.

Combine lime and orange juice in a bowl and whisk in the salad oil, salt and pepper until thickened. Pour into the salad and toss well.

Fruity Cabbage Salad

Ingredients

½ head small cabbage

1 cup grated carrot

2 tbsp chopped chives

2 to 3 slices fresh or canned pineapple, cut into chunks

⅓ cup lemon or lime juice

⅓ cup orange juice

½ cup salad oil

salt and pepper

2 tbsp pine nuts, toasted

Serves **4 people**

Arrange peppers, skin side up, on foil-covered baking trays. Cook under a hot grill or in the oven until skins are blistered, but not blackened. Turn as necessary. Place in a plastic bag for 10-15 minutes. When cool enough to handle, skin. Cut into ½ in/2cm squares.

Bring chicken stock to a boil, add peppers, tomato paste, and paprika. Season and add Tobasco sauce to taste. Add rice and simmer gently for 15 minutes or until rice is tender.

Pour the soup, in batches, into a food processor or blender and process until smooth. Reheat in sauce-pan. Garnish each serving with chives, serve with herbed bread.

Ingredients

4-5 large red or yellow peppers, halved

8 cups chicken stock

1 tbsp tomato paste

1 tsp ground black pepper

a few drops of Tobasco sauce

4 tbsp rice (uncooked)

¼ bunch chives

Roasted Pepper Soup

Serves **4 people**

Preheat oven to 400°F/ 200°C. Brush two oven trays with oil. Cut tops and bottoms off pepper. Cut lengthwise into quarters and flatten on baking trays, skin-side up. Roast for 12-15 minutes or until softened. Put into a plastic bag and leave to steam.

Roast the onion on a separate tray until golden. Leave to cool at the same time. When peppers are cool enough to handle, skin and cut into large chunky pieces.

Toss peppers and onions together in a shallow serving bowl. Top with anchovies (optional) and capers. Scatter with oregano and pepper and drizzle with combined oil and vinegar.

Roasted Pepper Salad

Ingredients

4 large peppers, red, yellow, and green
(if yellow are unavailable use more red than green)
1 purple onion, peeled and cut in thin slices from top to bottom
8 anchovy fillets, drained (optional)
1 tbsp capers, drained
¼ cup fresh oregano, chopped
ground black pepper to taste
2 tsp balsamic vinegar
2 tbsp olive oil

Serves **4–6 people**

Cut the cauliflower into florets, dice the potatoes and set aside. Heat oil in a wok or frypan. Fry seeds until they begin to pop. Add chili, garlic, ginger, turmeric, then ground cumin, then cook for 1 minute, stirring.

Add potato, cook while tossing for a few minutes. Add cauliflower and cook while tossing for a minute to coat with the spices. Add water, cover, and cook on low heat for 10 minutes or until the vegetables are tender.

Transfer to a serving dish. Add chicken stock to pan and cook until reduced by half. Pour over cauliflower and potato and serve.

Ingredients

1lb 2oz/500g cauliflower, cut into florets
1lb 2oz/500g potato, peeled and cut into ½in/2cm pieces
3 tbsp vegetable oil
1 tsp black mustard seeds
½ tsp whole cumin seeds
1 tsp freshly chopped chili
1 tsp freshly crushed garlic
½ tsp freshly chopped ginger
1 tsp ground turmeric
1 tsp ground cumin
¼ cup water
½ cup chicken stock

Spicy Cauliflower and Potato

Serves **4 people**

To make sauce: combine wine stock and herbs in a small saucepan. Bring to a boil then turn heat to low and simmer uncovered for 15 to 20 minutes to reduce by half. Remove from heat and stir in the cream, salt, and pepper. Return to heat and simmer 5 to 8 minutes more, stirring occasionally. Set the oven to 200°C/400°F

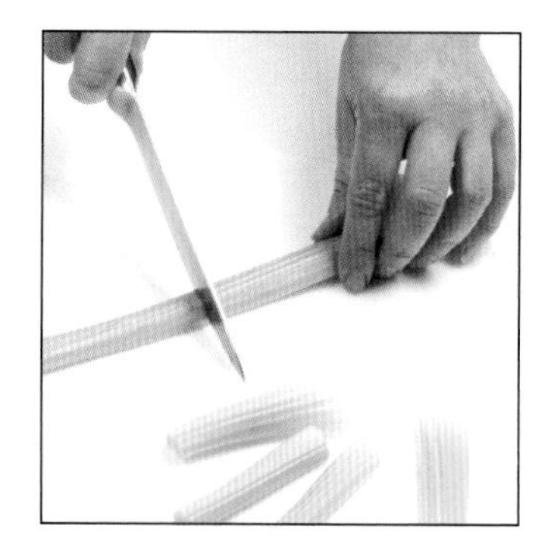

Separate the celery stalks, trim off the leaves and base and cut into 2in/8 cm length. Split wider pieces in half. Wash stalks well. Bring a large saucepan of salted water to a boil, add celery and cook for 10-15 minutes until almost tender. Drain immediately.

Grease an ovenproof dish with some of the butter. Arrange the celery in the dish and pour over the sauce. Cover with the fresh breadcrumbs and dot with remaining butter. Place in preheated oven and bake 20 to 30 minutes until browned.

Baked Celery with Herb Sauce

Ingredients

1 large or 2 small bunches of celery

2 tsp salt

⅓ cup butter

1 cup fresh breadcrumbs

Sauce

½ cup white wine

¾ cup thickened cream

2 tsp chopped parsley

2 tsp sweet basil leaves

1 tsp chopped chives

¼–⅓ cup chicken stock

salt and pepper to taste

Serves **6 people**

Preheat oven to 350°F/ 180°C. Peel chayote and cut into quarters. Steam or boil for 10 minutes until just tender. Drain.

Place the cooked chayote in a greased ovenproof dish. Combine the tomato and basil sauce, oregano, Tabasco sauce, and pepper and spoon over the chayote.

Sprinkle the top with breadcrumbs and dot with butter. Bake for 30 minutes or until golden. Serve immediately.

Ingredients

3 chayote

4oz/125g mozzarella, thinly sliced

1 cup prepared Tomato and Basil Sauce

1 tsp dried oregano leaves

a few drops Tobasco sauce (optional)

1 cup fresh breadcrumbs

3 tbsp butter

Chayote with Italian Tomato Sauce

Serves **4 people**

Remove the husks and silky threads from the corn, trim off the base. Place in saucepan of boiling water and cook until tender. Drain and serve hot with savory butter of your choice.

Place the butter in a bowl, heat with a wooden spoon until smooth. Mix in the respective flavoring ingredients.

Place each savory butter into a small pot and refrigerate until needed.

Corn on the Cob with Savory Butter

Ingredients

fresh corn cob (1 per person, steamed, boiled, microwaved, or barbecued)

Pepper butter

4oz/120g butter, at room temperature

2-3 slices grilled pepper, skinned and finely chopped

1 tsp dried chopped chives

1 tsp lemon juice

Savory butter

4oz/120g butter

1½ tsp ground coriander seeds

1 tsp ground cumin

1 tsp freshly chopped chili

Serves **4–6 people**

Cut the eggplant in half lengthwise and scoop out some of the flesh to create a shallow hollow. Finely chop the removed flesh. Saute the onions in hot oil until soft, add chopped flesh and saute 1 minute. Place in a bowl and stir in the chopped parsley, basil, tomatoes, salt, and pepper.

Heat oil and butter in the frying pan, add garlic and saute a little. Add the bread-crumbs, and stir constantly until all crumbs are coated. Remove from heat. Preheat oven to 350°F/180°C and oil a baking dish

Brush eggplants with oil and pack in the filling, mounding the top evenly. Press the breadcrumbs all over the top. Place in the baking dish and add water. Cover with a sheet of aluminium foil, and bake for 1 hour in preheated oven. Remove foil and bake until crumbs are browned.

Stuffed Eggplant

Ingredients

3 small-medium eggplants
¼ cup olive oil
2 large onions, finely chopped
¾ cup chopped fresh flat-leaf parsley
½ cup chopped fresh basil
4-5 ripe tomatoes, chopped
salt and pepper
1 tbsp olive oil
1 tbsp butter
2 tsp freshly crushed garlic
2 cups soft white breadcrumbs
Glad Roaster Pan

Serves **4–6 people**

Peel the cucumber and cut in half. Cut each half lengthwise. Place cut side down on chopping board, make 4 cuts lengthwise, then slice crosswise to form small cubes. Place cubes in a bowl and stir in the salt. Stand for 15-20 minutes.

Strain the liquid, pressing with the back of a spoon to extract as much water as possible.

Combine the yogurt, garlic, and vinegar in a bowl, stir in the drained cucumber, salt, and pepper. Cover and chill until needed. Just before serving, sprinkle with parsley or mint. Serve with crackers or pita bread.

Cucumber in Yogurt

Ingredients

1 telegraph or 2–3 Lebanese cucumbers

1 tsp salt

1⅓ cup/10oz/300 ml natural yogurt

1 tsp freshly crushed garlic

1 tsp white wine vinegar

white pepper

1 tbsp fresh parsley or mint, chopped

Serves **4–6 people**

Wash the fennel well and trim off the base and all of the green stalks. Melt the butter in a large saucepan, add the fennel, onion, and garlic and stir to coat well. Cover, turn down the heat to low and allow to sweat for 10-15 minutes to soften.

With a pointed knife, slash through the tomatoes while in the cans, then tip the tomatoes and juice into the fennel. Season with salt, pepper, and oregano. Bring to a boil, turn down the heat and simmer, uncovered, for 30 minutes.

Puree in 2 or 3 batches in a food processor or blender. Return to the saucepan. Add chicken stock and Pernod. Bring back to a boil over high heat, turn down and simmer 2 minutes. Serve hot with a sprinkling of grated Parmesan cheese and crusty bread.

Ingredients

1lb 2oz/1kg fennel bulbs
1 large onion, chopped roughly
2 tsp freshly crushed garlic
2 cans peeled tomtoes
(approximately 14oz/400 grams each)

2½ cups chicken stock
2 tsp oregano leaves
2oz/60g butter
¼ cup Pernod (optional)
salt and ground black pepper to taste

Fennel and Tomato Soup

Serves **4 people**

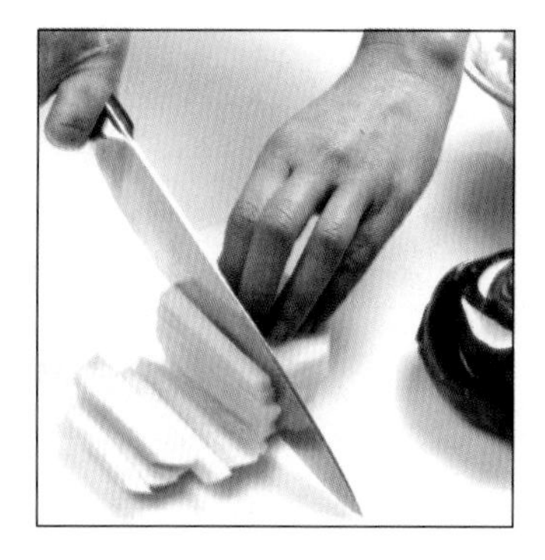

Cut the base off the kohlrabi, trim off the stalks and peel. Cut crosswise into ¼in/5 mm slices, then cut each slice into 5 mm wide batons.

Place in a wide based saucepan with enough boiling salted water to just cover. Cover and boil 2-3 minutes.
Drain well.

Heat the butter in the saucepan, add the kohlrabi and toss well to coat. Add the cream and simmer uncovered for 5 minutes until the cream has thickened enough to coat the batons. Add the dill, chives, and lemon juice.
Toss to distribute.

Kohlrabi with Creamy Dill Sauce

Ingredients

8 kohlrabi (cabbage turnip), trimmed, peeled thick

3 tbsp butter

½ cup thickened cream

1 tsp snipped dill tips

1 tsp chopped chives

1 tbsp lemon juice.

Serves **4 people**

Wash leeks, cut out root end and green leaves. Dice 3 inside green leave for garnish. Leave the white parts whole and blanch in boiling salted water for 1 minute; remove.

Heat oil in a saucepan, toss in the diced greens and pepper and cook 5 minutes. Add the wine, lemon juice, zest, coriander, and herbs bring to a boil.

Add the white blanched leeks, cover, and simmer for 15-20 minutes. Transfer leeks to a serving dish and pour over the juices. Refrigerate, serve chilled with grilled chicken or fish.

Leek and Red Pepper

Ingredients

1lb 2oz/500g leeks

4 tbsp olive oil

1 large red pepper, seeded and diced

½ cup dry white wine

juice of ½ lemon

½ tsp lemon zest

8 coriander seeds

salt and pepper

1 bay leaf

2 sprigs parsley

2 sprigs coriander

Serves **4–6 people**

Cut the partially frozen beef fillet into ¼ in/5mm slices. Lay each slice on a board and cut, with the grain, into ¼ in/5mm strips.

Heat half the butter in a large heavy-based frying pan, add onion and saute until transparent and slightly colored. Add all beef strips and cook over high heat for a few minutes, tossing meat constantly with a spoon until lightly browned. Add sliced mushrooms and cook 2 minutes. Set aside, cover, and keep warm.

Melt remaining butter in a small saucepan, add flour and mustard and stir over heat for 1 minute. Gradually add beef stock and stir until it thickens. Remove from heat and stir in sour cream. Add salt and pepper, then pour into pan with meat. Reheat over gentle heat, but do not boil. Spoon meat onto a heated serving platter. Serve with potatoes or slim cut chips.

Beef Stroganoff

Ingredients

1lb 12oz/750g fillet of beef, trimmed

3 tbsp butter

1 onion, very thinly sliced

5½ oz/155g button mushrooms, thinly sliced

1½ tbsp plain flour

1 tsp dry mustard

1⅓ cups beef stock

½ cup sour cream

salt and pepper to taste

Serves **6–8 people**

Heat the butter and oil in a large saucepan and cook the onions over a low heat for 15 minutes. Add the salt and sugar. Cook for 30-40 minutes, stirring frequently, until the onions are a deep golden brown.

Add the flour and stir for 3 minutes. Meanwhile bring the stock to a boil. Remove onions from heat and gradually stir in the stock and wine. Season to taste with salt and pepper.

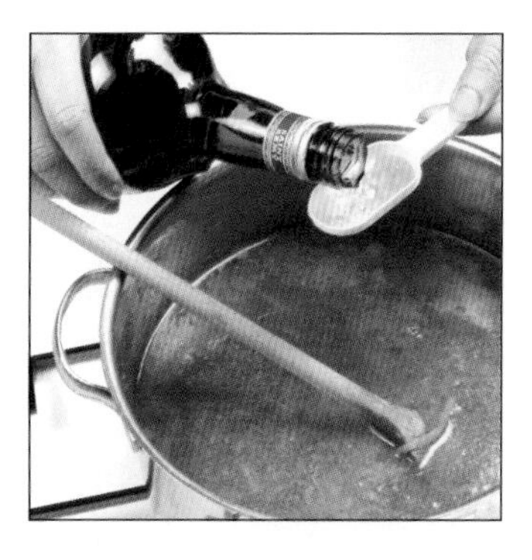

Simmer partially covered for 30-40 minutes, skimming occasionally. Adjust seasoning. Just before serving, stir in the cognac. Serve with rounds of French bread and a sprinkling of grated cheese, if desired.

Onion Soup

Ingredients

1lb 10oz/750g onion, thinly sliced

2oz/50g butter

1 tbsp oil

1 tsp salt

¼ tsp sugar

2 tbsp flour

4 cups beef stock, boiling

1¼ cups dry white wine

salt and pepper to taste

3 tbsp cognac or brandy

Serves **8 people**

Melt butter in a large frypan. Cook garlic 1 minute. Add parsnip and carrot and cook over medium heat, stirring occasionally, until almost cooked. Season with rosemary, parsley, and pepper.

Transfer to greased shallow ovenproof dish and pour over cream. Preheat oven to 400°F/200°C oven for 35 minutes or until browned.

Mix breadcrumbs and Parmesan together and sprinkle a thick layer over the top. Dot with butter and bake in a preheated oven for 35 minutes or until bronwed.

Parsnip and Carrot Bake

Ingredients

2oz/60g butter

1lb/500g parsnip, washed and grated

12oz/350g carrot, peeled and grated

1⅓ cup cream

ground black pepper to taste

1 tsp freshly crushed garlic

1½ cups fresh breadcrumbs

3 tbsp Parmesan cheese, grated

1 tsp rosemary leaves

1 tsp parsley flakes

Serves **6 people**

Saute onions in butter until softened. Add bacon. Cook for a few minutes, then add peas and stir.

Add 2¾ cups stock, cover, and simmer for 10 minutes. Add rice, parsley, and remaining stock. Cover and cook over low heat until rice is tender. Season with salt and pepper.

Toss through half the cheese. To serve, add Parmesan cheese separately.

Pea Risotto

Ingredients

1 medium onion, finely chopped

3 tbsp butter

2oz/50g bacon, chopped

2lb 4oz/1kg fresh peas, shelled

3 cups chicken stock

15oz/400g Italian Arborio rice

(if unavailable use calrose rice)

2 tsp parsley flakes

⅓ cup Parmesan cheese, grated

Serves **4 people**

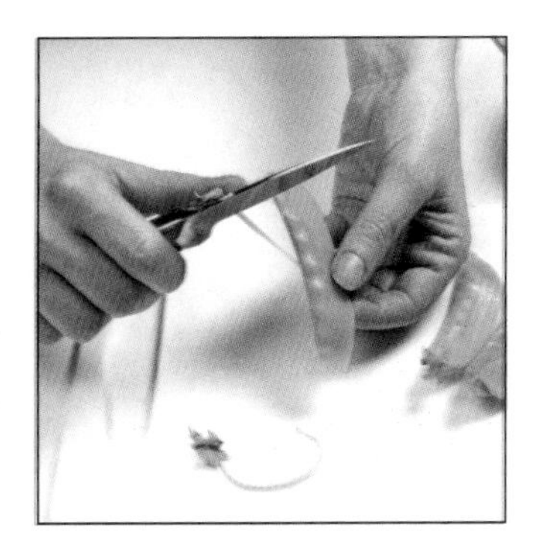

Rinse snow peas. Top and tail and remove the string. Cook snow peas in boiling water for 20 seconds until bright green. Drain and rinse under cold water.

Split along curved side, leaving straight side intact. Process remaining ingredients, except caviar, in a food processor. Using a piping bag, pipe mixture into snow peas.

Using a piping bag, pipe mixture into snow peas. Refrigerate until firm. Garnish with red caviar.

Snow Pea Savories

Ingredients

24 snow peas

4½ oz/125g cream cheese

2 tbsp fresh parsley, chopped

2 tsp fresh chives, chopped

pinch of ground cayenne pepper

1 small jar red caviar

Serves **4–6 people**

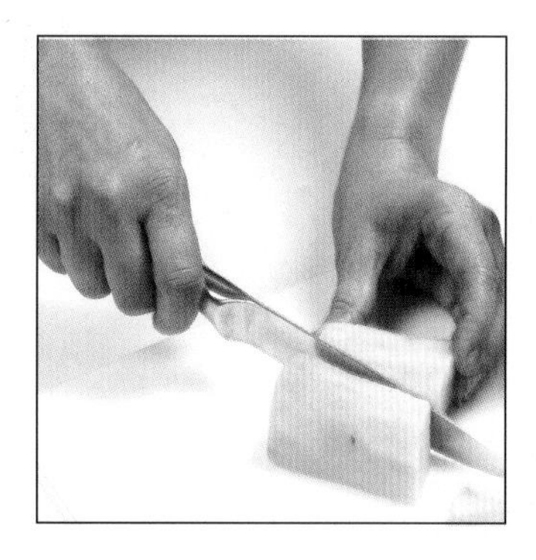

Peel potatoes and boil in water until almost cooked. Drain and cut into quarters.

Melt butter in a large frypan. Add sweet potatoes and sprinkle with the brown sugar and orange zest. Cook, turning occasionally, for about 6-7 minutes. In this time, the sugar should caramelise and form a crunchy coating over the potatoes.

Turn to coat the potatoes. Transfer to serving dish and serve.

Ingredients

1lb 12oz/750g white sweet potato

3 tbsp butter

½ cup brown sugar

1 tsp grated orange zest

Caramelised Sweet Potato

Serves **6 people**

Heat oil in a deep pot and fry the onions until soft along with the nutmeg and cardamom. Cook over medium heat for 5 minutes, stirring occasionally.

Add stock and bring to a boil. Reduce heat and cook until pumpkin is tender. Purée in a food processor or blender until smooth.

Return to pot. Add milk and heat, but do not boil. Serve hot with a dollop of sour cream and a sprinkling of chopped chives and ground pepper.

Pumpkin Soup

Ingredients

1 tbsp oil

1 medium onion, diced

1 potato, peeled and diced

2lb 4oz/1kg pumpkin, peeled and diced

4 cups chicken or vegetable stock

1 cup milk

½ tsp ground nutmeg

pinch ground cardamom

freshly ground black pepper to taste

sour cream and chives to serve

Serves **6 people**

Preheat oven to 380°F/190°C. Place thyme, basil, salt, and butter in a food processor and process for 10 seconds. With motor running, add the iced water to form a dough. Remove to a floured board and knead into a ball. Cover with plastic wrap and refrigerate 20 mins. Roll dough out on a floured board. Line raw shell with greased paper and fill with rice (blind bake) to prevent sides from collapsing. Bake for 10 minutes. Remove from oven and remove blind bake.

Filling: Heat oil in a frying pan, add onion and pepper and stir, lower heat, cover and cook slowly for 25-30 minutes, stirring occassionally. Uncover and cook to evaporate any juices. spoon filling into flan case

Topping: Cut the tomatoes into 4 lengthwise, remove seeds. Arrange skin-side up in a decorative pattern with garlic slices, oil, pepper, thyme, and basil. Bake in preheated oven 380°F/190°C for 30-35 minutes. Stand 10 minutes before serving.

Tomato Flan

Ingredients

Tomato flan

1 ¼ cups flour

1 tsp thyme leaves

1 tsp sweet basil leaves

¾ cup butter, cut into cubes

2 tbsp iced water

½ tsp salt

Filling

2 tbsp olive oil

4 red peppers, cut into strips

1 medium onion sliced

ground black pepper

Topping

5 ripe plum tomatoes

15 kalamata olives, pitted and halved

4 cloves garlic, thinly sliced

1 tsp thyme leaves

1 tsp sweet basil leaves

2 tbsp oil

Serves **4 people**

Saute onion in oil for 5 minutes. Add carrot, salt, rutabaga, and pepper. Saute for 10 minutes, stirring occasionally.

Add vegetable stock and cook covered over low heat for 20-30 minutes until vegetables are tender.

Add spices. Puree in a food processor with orange juice. Reheat and serve.

Ingredients

1 medium onion, diced

1 peeled and chopped rutabaga (about 2 cups)

3 small carrots, peeled and chopped

1 cup vegetable stock

½ tsp ground ginger

¼ tsp ground nutmeg

2 cups fresh orange juice

freshly ground black pepper to taste

1 tbsp oil

salt to taste

Rutabaga and Carrot Soup

Serves **4 people**

Trim a little from one end of the potato so they will stand upright in a baking dish. Trim a larger portion from the other end and set aside.

Scoop out the flesh of the potato. Grate or finely chop and combine with the salt, pepper, rosemary, garlic, onion, butter, and half of the cheese. Fill the potatoes with this mixture and place the potato lid back on top.

Stand potatoes in a baking tray that has been lined with a sheet of baking paper. Brush the potatoes with a little oil. Bake in a 350°F/180°C oven for 45 minutes to 1 hour. Sprinkle with remaining grated cheese and serve with sour cream and a sprinkle of paprika.

Stuffed Baked Potatoes

Ingredients

4 large potatoes, scrubbed

salt and pepper

1 tsp rosemary leaves

1 tsp freshly crushed garlic

1 small onion, diced

3½ cup/100g Gruyere cheese, grated

3 tbsp butter

vegetable oil

Serves **4–6 people**

Place grated zucchini in a colander and sprinkle with salt. Leave to drain for ½-1 hour. Squeeze out all moisture.

Heat oil in a frypan. Add zucchini and cook for 5 minutes or until tender, stirring occasionally.

Add lemon juice and herbs and mix through. Season with pepper and serve.

Ingredients

2lb 4oz/1kg zucchini, grated

2 tbsp olive oil

2 tsp lemon juice

1 tbsp fresh basil

1 tbsp fresh marjoram

1 tbsp fresh parsley

freshly ground black pepper

salt

Zucchini with Herbs

Serves **4–6 people**

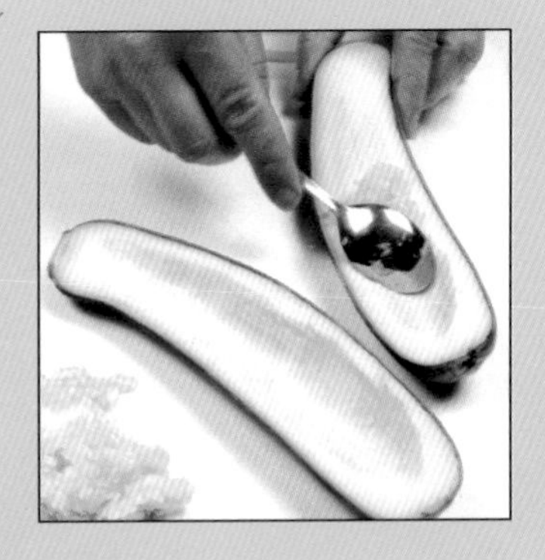

Wash zucchini and cut in half lengthwise. Scoop out the seeds and a little of the flesh using a teaspoon.

Place the flesh from zucchini and remaining ingredients in a bowl and mix well. Preheat oven to 380°F/190°C

Fill the zucchini halves with filling. Place on a lightly oiled baking tray and bake in preapred oven for 20 minutes until tender and browned.

Stuffed Zucchini

Ingredients

6 medium zucchini

4 tbsp bacon, finely chopped

4 tbsp bolognese sauce

2 small tomatoes, seeds removed and diced

4 tbsp breadcrumbs

5 tbsp Parmesan cheese, grated

2 tsp chopped parsley

½ tsp oregano leaves

freshly ground black pepper

salt

Serves **4 people**

Preheat oven to 400°F/200°C. Halve endives lengthwise and slice thinly lengthwise. Melt two tablespoons of the butter in a frypan. Cook endives for about 8 minutes stirring frequently until they are tender and liquid has evaporated. Remove from heat and stir in half the lime juice.

Melt 1 tablespoon butter in a frying pan and saute 8 scallops 30 seconds each side or until cooked. Remove.

Combine the remaining lime juice and wine in a saucepan and bring to a boil. Reduce heat and gradually whisk in the remaining 4 tablespoons butter. Remove from heat and season with pepper and lime zest. To serve, reheat endives and divide food between 4 serving plates. Place 4 scallops on each plate. Sprinkle with pepper and spoon over the sauce.

Scallops with Belgian Endive

Ingredients

6 large Belgian endive

6 tbsp butter

3 tbsp lime or lemon juice

1 tsp lime or lemon zest, grated

1 ½ tbsp dry white wine

freshly ground black pepper

16 large scallops

Serves **6 people**

Trim rind from bacon and fry until very crisp. Remove from pan, crumble, and set aside.

Cook the garlic, onion, and okra in the bacon fat. Add corn kernels and cook for 10 minutes, stirring continuously.

Add tomatoes, pepper, sugar, salt, chili, and oregano. Cover and simmer for 25 minutes. Transfer to a serving dish and top with crumbled bacon.

Okra, Corn, and Tomato Braise

Ingredients

4 slices bacon

7oz/200g okra

4 corncobs, kernels removed

3 large tomatoes, peeled and roughly chopped

1 onion, finely chopped

1 green pepper

1 tsp freshly crushed garlic

1 tsp sugar

1 tsp freshly chopped chili

1 tsp oregano leaves

Serves **4 people**

Heat oil in a wok or frypan. When it is very hot, add the garlic, chili, and spring onion, cook for a few minutes. Reduce heat, add chicken and stir-fry for 2 min.

Add the soy sauce and stock and bring to a boil. Add the broccoli and mushrooms and stir fry-for 3 minutes over medium heat until the broccoli has reduced in bulk.

Move meat and vegetables to one side, add the cornflour paste and allow to sit in order to thicken. Toss vegetables and chicken to coat with sauce. Serve immediately.

Ingredients

2 tbsp oil

3 tsp freshly crushed garlic

1 chili, finely sliced

5 spring onions, finely sliced

6oz/180g chicken thigh or breast fillets, finely sliced

1 tbsp soy sauce

⅓ cup chicken stock

14oz/400g Chinese broccoli, washed, trimmed and sliced

4oz/100g oyster mushrooms

2 tsp cornflour made into a paste with some water

Chicken with Chinese Broccoli

Serves **4 people**

Heat oil in wok or frypan, add ginger, garlic, and onion and fry for 1 minute. Add pepper, beans, and pineapple. Fry for 1 minute, remove from wok.

Heat extra oil in wok, add sauces then ¼ of the chicken, stir-fry for for a few minutes or until chicken is tender. Remove from wok. Continue to fry remaining chicken in the same way. Return vegetables and chicken to the wok.

Blend cornflour and water, add to pan with vegetables and chicken, stir-fry until mixture boils and thickens. Serve with steamed rice.

Chicken and Pineapple Stir-Fry

Ingredients

1 tbsp oil
1 tsp freshly chopped ginger
1 tsp freshly crushed garlic
1 medium onion, sliced
1 red pepper, sliced
9oz/250g green beans, sliced
1 small pineapple, peeled and chopped
1 tbsp oil, extra
1 tbsp oyster sauce
2 tsp chili sauce (optional)
1lb 2oz/500g chicken thigh fillets, sliced
2 tsp cornflour
2 tbsp water.

Serves **4 people**

Butterfly the shrimp, cutting along the inner curve, ¾ of the way through. Open out, remove the vein and flatten by pressing down with side of a large knife.

Dip each shrimp into the seasoned flour then into the beaten egg to coat both sides. Place onto the coconut mixture, covering all sides, and pressing down lightly for the mixture to adhere. Place the shrimp on a flat oven tray and refrigerate 20 minutes or more.

Heat the butter or olive oil in a frying pan, add shrimp and fry each side until golden over a high heat for 1-2 minutes. (You may need to apply pressure with a spatula as they cook to prevent them from curling up).

Combine mango, onion, coriander, and lime juice in a bowl, then season to taste. Arrange some salad greens on each plate before serving and top with 3 pieces of shrimp and a generous spoonful of the mango salsa. Drizzle over any remaining salsa juice and serve immediately with lime wedges (if desired).

Ingredients

12 raw king shrimp, peeled (tails on)

seasoned flour for dusting

1 egg, beaten

5oz/155g sesame seeds

3oz/90g shredded coconut

1 mango, peeled and finely diced

½ small spanish onion, finely diced

2 tbsp chopped coriander

juice of 1 lime

2 tbsp butter or olive oil

5oz/150g mixed salad greens of your choice

lime quarters for garnish

King Shrimp with Mango Salsa

Serves **4 people**

Mix together the eggs, sugar, flour, and salt. Put enough oil in pan to reach a height of ½ in/1½ cm.

Heat oil in the frying pan. Dip the apple pieces into the batter and fry them in the hot oil until golden.

Drain the fritters on kitchen paper. Sprinkle with powdered sugar and serve immediately.

Ingredients

4 apples, peeled, cored, and sliced into 5mm rings

vegetable oil for deep frying

powdered sugar for dusting

2 eggs

1 tbsp sugar

3 tbsp flour

pinch salt

Apple Fritters

Serves **6 people**

Grease an ovenproof dish with butter. Peel the bananas and arrange on the dish. Mix brown sugar, cinnamon, and ginger together and sprinkle over the bananas.

Mix the orange juice and Cointreau together and spoon over the bananas

Dot surface with knobs of butter. Bake in a preheated oven 375°F/190°C for 20 minutes basting occasionally. Serve warm with thickened or whipped cream or ice cream.

Baked Bananas

Ingredients

6 large bananas

4 tbsp brown sugar

1 tsp ground cinnamon

1 tsp ground ginger

¾ cup orange juice

¼ cup Cointreau

1 tbsp butter

Serves **8 people**

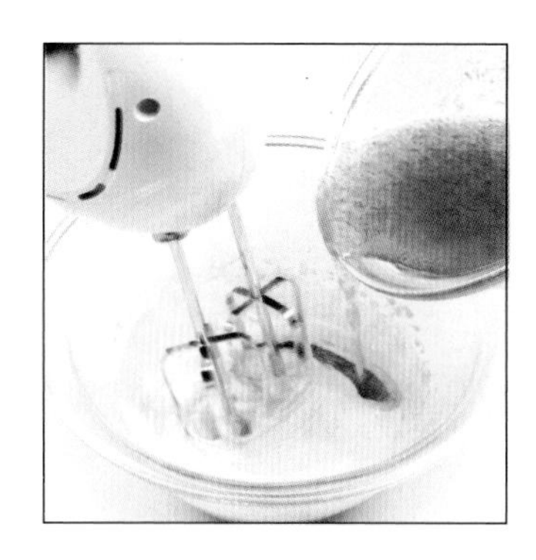

Prepare the syrup, combine the water and sugar in a small saucepan, and stir until boiling. Turn down heat, add the lime zest and simmer until reduced by half, about 25-30 minutes. Remove from heat and sprinkle in the gelatin, stir to dissolve. To prepare the crust: combine all ingredients in a bowl, mix well. Press into the base of a 9½ in/24 cm spring form pan. Refrigerate

Beat eggyolks and ¼ cup sugar in a bowl, until thick and frothy. Gradually beat in the syrup and the lime juice. Return mixture to the saucepan and stir over low heat until custard consistency. Allow to cool.

Stiffly beat the egg whites, gradually add remaining ¼ cup sugar until meringue consistency. Fold the whipped cream gently into the egg whites drizzling in the lime custard mixture as you gently fold. Spoon onto the prepared crust and smooth over. Refrigerate for 2-3 hours until set.

Key Lime Pie

Ingredients

Syrup

1 cup water

½ cup sugar

2 tbsp grated lime zest

Crumb crust

2 cups plain sweet biscuit crumbs

7oz/200g butter, melted

2 tsp grated lime zest

Filling

1 envelope unflavored gelatin

⅓ cup fresh lime juice

½ cup caster sugar

2 eggs, separated

1 cup cream

1 tsp vanilla essence

Serves **6–8 people**

Put sugar, egg, butter and milk into food processor and blend until butter is in small pieces. Add flour and process to blend.

Remove from bowl and kneed lightly to form a smooth ball. Wrap in plastic wrap and place in refrigerator for 1 hour to rest.

Arrange dates in base of pastry case. Beat egg yolks, sugar, and vanilla together then stir in the cream. Pour into the pastry case. Bake in oven at 375°F/180°C for 25 minutes or until custard is just set. It will thicken more upon cooling.

Date Tart

Ingredients

Pastry

6oz/180g butter, cut into cubes

3 tbsp caster sugar

1 egg

1 tbsp milk

2 cups plain flour

Filling

10 fresh dates, halved and pitted

4 large egg yolks

2 tbsp caster sugar

¾ cup cream

1 tsp vanilla

Serves **4 people**

Slice the top off the melon or vandyke by making "v" cuts around the melon. Scoop out the seeds with a small, sharp knife, and discard. Cut a thin slice off the base to stabilize.

Spoon the flesh out in large chunks with a large spoon and cut into bite-sized pieces

Place melon pieces and other prepared fruits in a large bowl. Mix juices, sugar, vermouth, and liqueur together, pour over fruit and toss gently to mix through. Spoon into the melon shell. Chill before serving.

Fruit-filled Honeydew

Ingredients

1 honeydew melon

2 peaches, peeled, stoned, and chopped

7oz/200g cherries or grapes

juice of 1 lemon

juice of 1 orange

2 tbsp sweet white vermouth

1 tbsp orange liqueur

3 tbsp sugar

Serves **6–8 people**

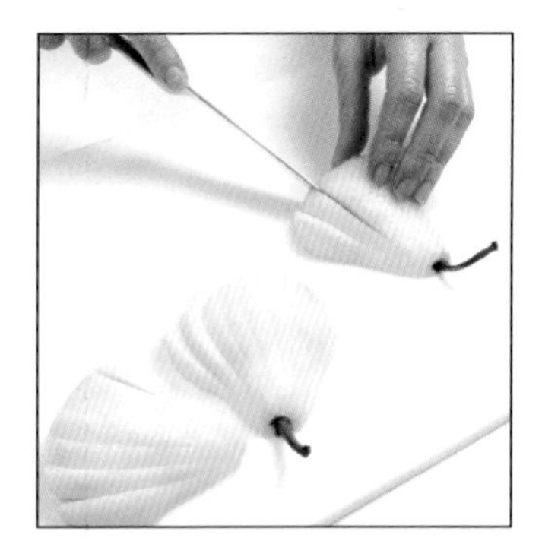

Halve the pears lengthwise and remove core. Place cut side down on a board and make 5-6 cuts ½ in/2cm from top stem end.

Place the pears into a buttered oven dish and fan the slices out a little. Add the cinnamon sticks and cloves, then sprinkle each pear with combined brown sugar, cinnamon, and nutmeg. Dot the pears with butter and bake in preheated oven 375°F/180°C for 20-25 minutes.

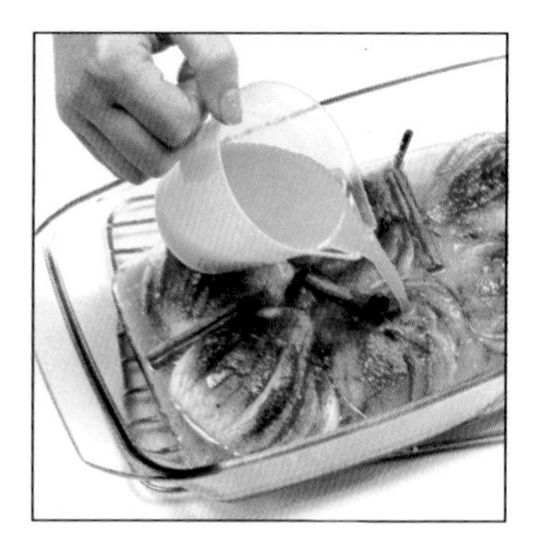

Remove pears from the oven and pour over the rum or orange juice. Return to oven for 5 minutes. Serve warm with cream.

Fragrant Baked Pears

Ingredients

3 firm ripe pears, peeled

4 cinnamon sticks

2 whole cloves

1 ½ tsp ground cinnamon

½ tsp ground nutmeg

2 tbsp unsalted butter, cut into cubes

¾ cup dark rum or orange juice

4 tbsp brown sugar

Serves **6–8 people**

Scoop out the seeds from the pawpaw, peel, cut, and dice. Wash and cut remaining fruit.

Place all the prepared fruits into a large glass bowl. Mix gently with gloved hands so as not to bruise the fruit.

Pour lemon juice over the fruit salad, this will bring out the flavor of the pawpaw. Pour over Grand Marnier or other liquer. Serve chilled.

Pawpaw Fruit Salad

Ingredients

½ pawpaw or papaya

2 oranges, cut into segments

3 kiwis, sliced

small bunch white grapes

small bunch red grapes

pulp of 2 passionfruits

1 banana, sliced

¼ pineapple, cut into small pieces

1 box strawberries

6 mint leaves

juice of 1 lemon

3 tbsp Grand Marnier or other liqueur

Carrot Cake

Serves **8 people**

Preheat oven to 350°F/ 180°C. In a bowl, sift the flour, baking powder, baking soda, salt, cinnamon, and sugar. Form a well in the center and add beaten eggs and oil. Stir to form a batter. Stir in the carrot, pineapple, and walnuts.

Grease a loaf tin and line the base with oiled paper. Pour in the cake mixture. Bake in preheated oven for 35-40 minutes. Turn out onto a cake rack to cool.

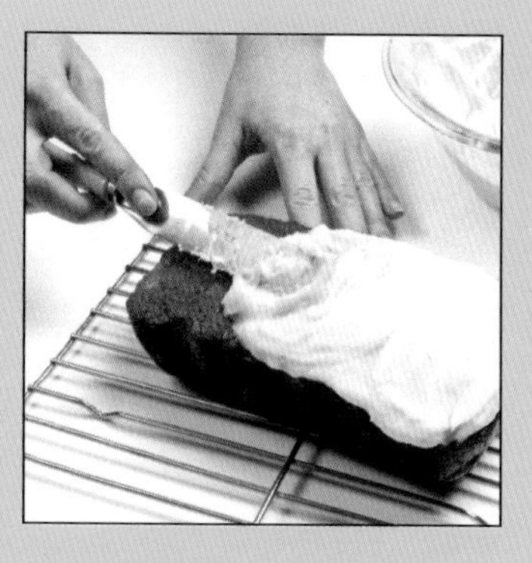

Place all ingredients in a bowl for the icing and beat well. If it is too thick, add a little milk. Spread over top of cake and decorate with walnut halves.

Ingredients

1 cup plain flour

1 tsp baking powder

¾ tsp baking soda

½ tsp salt

½ tsp ground cinnamon

¾ cup sugar

2 eggs lightly beaten

½ cup vegetable oil

1 cup grated carrot

7oz/200g canned, crushed pineapple, drained of juice

¼ cup chopped walnuts

Icing

3 tbsp butter

3 tbsp cream cheese

½ tsp vanilla

2 cups powdered sugar

walnut halves to decorate

Serves **6 people**

Place a layer of apples into a 10in/20 cm cake pan or baking dish and sprinkle with some of the lemon juice. Repeat the layers until all the apples are in the pan.

Process the flour, sugar, and cinnamon in a food processor and combine. Add the butter, using repeated pulses until the mixture resembles coarse breadcrumbs.

Sprinkle the crumb mixture over the apples. Bake for 1 hour at 350°F/175°C. Serve warm with cream, ice-cream, or custard.

Ingredients

5 granny smith apples, peeled, cored, and thinly sliced

2 tbsp fresh lemon juice

1 cup plain flour

1 cup sugar

1½ tsp cinnamon

5oz/125g butter, cold, cut into pieces

Apple Crumble

Index